MW00982284

DEPRESSION'S DANCE

May all your tears be from Laughter

Hasty

WRITTEN BY
HASTYWORDS

Depression's Dance

Copyright © 2013 by HastyWords, All rights reserved.

This book is about my dance with depression. I am not a medical professional and what I write is simply from my point of view. If I have learned anything, it is that depression is sneaky. It isn't an emotion; it isn't a state of mind; it is a disease. My advice, if you think you might be depressed: find someone to talk to and acknowledge it before it tries to kill you.

DEDICATED TO THE MANY WHO DANCE WITH DEPRESSION AND NEVER GIVE UP!

ααα

MY NAME IS HASTY

I can't exactly pinpoint how or when it happened, but one day I woke up feeling broken. Somewhere I made a wrong turn and my life didn't look like mine anymore. I was a working professional by day, a 40 year old wife and mom during the week, and acting like I was in my twenties on weekends. I had all I had ever dreamed of having, but something was wrong.

In the beginning, I wasn't sure if I wanted anyone to know how I felt. It was my smile people wanted to see, not my tears. People naturally gravitate towards positive attitudes and I didn't want to be the negative energy they avoided. But eventually the tears come and there is nothing you can do to hinder them. The tears have a story to tell and they won't stop until they have their say.

I decided to let them write...

MY NAME IS DEPRESSION

It is getting late, but stick around, because tonight I will help her destroy herself.

I have been attacking her quietly for a few years. Lack of sleep, along with the notion she is completely oblivious to my existence, makes her easy to control. To her I am just a mood… a storm of emotions that she is prone to feeling. I am neither a mood nor an emotion.

The biggest lie she tells herself is that she can control me. Hahaha. It tickles me; such an innocent thing to believe yet wholly dangerous to underestimate me that way. I hope you don't feel sorry for her because she isn't the only one that doesn't acknowledge me. You see, it is my job to destroy humanity one person at a time by being undetected. I am a demon you can call depression and I am pretty effective at my job.

I am looking forward to channeling all my anticipation into this last night with her. Tonight I am restless and she is mine one last time before I claim victory.

THE STORM IS COMING

DEPRESSION'S VOICE:

LOL you like to describe me as a storm. I have to say it is my favorite way to be described. A good storm is a beautifully powerful thing to watch and so easily destructive.

Oh, and this breathing thing, people seem to think being able to breathe makes them so special. Breathing is over–rated. It is the one thing I take pleasure in taking away and I am looking forward to the day I take away yours.

THE STORM IS COMING

The storm is coming
My body feels it
The cloudy darkness
Settling in my brain
And when I say darkness
I mean the heavy inky kind
That covers everything
Dammit not again
Deep breaths in…out
Slow…10 of them
Think only of the breath
Open my eyes…dark
Maybe more than 10
Close my eyes
Don't think just breathe
I am the breath
I am long, solid, peaceful breaths
Deep, healthy, positive breaths
Open my eyes…dark
I sigh in resignation
Buckle myself in
Prepare for the ride
Close my eyes
And hope when I open them
There is something of me left

A LITTLE FRIENDLY ADVICE

HASTY'S VOICE:

I don't understand why, during certain moments, I say one thing when I mean the total opposite. Why when I am hurting do I not just come out and say "I need help?" I think I want a friend to come hold my hand and talk with me, but I don't know what to say about how I feel. I don't want to ask for help because I am better at giving it. I think what I want is to know someone is willing to stop what they are doing and just talk to me, redirect my fears and my anxieties, and pay attention to me. But maybe not. I don't know what I really want. If I don't know how can anyone else know?

Part of me wants to be ok and have the selfless feelings and thoughts that portray strength and courage, but the other side is desperate and weak. Here I sit alone crying on the stairs fighting to find some sort of sanity…some reason. I am going to text a few friends that know I have a dark side. My friends don't need to know when I need space…I would just take it. But here I am texting some random nonsense.

A LITTLE FRIENDLY ADVICE

Dear friends, I am not well

Please help me I am desperate as hell

I need some time and space

I need to know I am important to you

I do not want to feel

Well this is honest at least

Just know I love you in my silence

Do you feel the same?

And don't worry I will be ok

I am such a liar, I am so not ok

Dear Friend, I love you

Really? I desperately need it!

Thanks love you too

I am here for you if you need me

Where is here? Not sure what I need

Thanks that means a lot

I want you to feel better, praying for you

Yes, pray.. like literally right now

Thank you

I love you and really think you need to get help

Ask me what is wrong….please, I mean
I
don't have an answer but ask anyway

I am going to…thank you

You need to do what is best for you

Yea, I guess…I mean can you tell me
what
that is?

I know I am working on it

BARRELING DOWN THE SPEEDWAY

HASTY'S VOICE:

I imagine my thoughts like a speedway. Emotions barreling so fast all anyone can do is stand back and watch, cheering me on from the sidelines.

BARRELING DOWN THE SPEEDWAY

My life, my life, my life

A story, a reality, a fiction inside my head

It is a work in process unfolding, unstopping

Beginnings and endings alternating

Speed writing, speed reading, speed thinking

Thoughts racing on a one way track

I can see the conclusion

Brace myself for the multiple collision crash

Taking myself and my loved ones with me

Anxiety builds at the loss of control

I grip the wheel and pray silently

Then a bell rings…distant at first

Pit stop calling me, signaling me in

I hear the voice if not the words

Over all the noise and know I am not alone

Moving too fast before to read the signs

I begin to notice more than just the voice

A group of people standing by

Cheering me on to the finish line

I AM NOT OK

DEPRESSION'S VOICE:

This is never good. You still don't know who you are dealing with but you are starting to ask questions, finally admitting you don't understand. Once you reach out for help my job becomes much harder. Looks like I am going to be putting in a bit of overtime on you.

I AM NOT OK

I don't want to linger with these thoughts very long. I know I have to concentrate on me. Writing my thoughts, getting in touch with my emotions feels weak and I don't like its bitter taste. I can see now that these feelings are definitely NOT ok. What these feelings do to those I love is NOT ok. These revelations were slow to be realized and owned up to.

You see, I have an image to uphold. I don't really, but in my mind I do. I am strong, the person who accepts a challenge and succeeds. I have finally realized I can't keep pretending...the feelings that have been leaking out in different forms over the last year or so have become a hemorrhage. They have been slowly tearing down my marriage and my most cherished friendships. I can control the damage...I can finally admit I am not capable of dealing with everything. I am not invincible...dang it.

At this point, I can't worry about how people will react to discovering I am an emotional mess. I can only hope my story will serve some sort of purpose.

AGAIN... AGAIN... AGAIN

DEPRESSION'S VOICE:

UGH... This kid of yours likes to unravel hours of my work with her smile. When someone has kids, the trick is to make them feel they are letting them down.

AGAIN... AGAIN... AGAIN

Woke up looking for myself **AGAIN**. I could feel reality playing hide-n-seek in my mind **AGAIN**. Desperately trying to find any evidence I had been there, a trail, breadcrumbs, anything **AGAIN**. A clue that might help me find my confidence before the insecurities, in this absence of reality, come out and play and run rampant **AGAIN**. I jump in the shower because many times this is where I find myself **AGAIN**. But like many other times it doesn't work **AGAIN**. I hurry to find myself in music and sit listening to Michael Buble sing to me about a new day, a new dawn, and a new life and I hope to be feeling good **AGAIN**. Apparently, today it isn't going to be easy **AGAIN**. The happy, optimistic, fearless, loving, part of me has been bullied deep into the alleyways of my mind **AGAIN**. As I look outside I realize the clouds in the sky are bullying the sun **AGAIN**. I worry all hope for finding myself today are lost when I hear the most beautiful voice say, "Hey, Good morning mom!" and like many times before I find myself in her eyes **AGAIN**.

STOLEN MOMENTS

DEPRESSION'S VOICE:

The funny thing about you, Hasty, is that you see me in other people but you can't see me in yourself.

STOLEN MOMENTS

Sometimes I wonder if he could utter the words that could save his life. I have never seen someone so full of pain and sadness and it kills any words I might utter in return. Depression is a thief stealing perfectly good moments and locking them in the dark. There must have been dreams and hopes once upon a time. I have spent so much time growing old with him wondering how I can help if only to share happiness in the very last of our minutes. I used to believe it was completely up to me to create the joy. Beyond exhaustion, I grasp at the last of my power for the super human strength it will take to chase the clouds away. Whispering in his ear and scratching his back I have only the words, **"I love you and I am always here!"**.

FRUSTRATED RESOLVE

HASTY'S VOICE:

I find myself very easily annoyed and frustrated these days. This is a big deal because my feathers were never easily ruffled. Maybe it is old age, or constant busyness, or just not enough time to sit and reflect. Regardless, I find that being frustrated is a contagious condition and maybe I just had a really good immunity to it before the last year or so. The following was written in two parts... I wrote the first part on my phone as a note during my frustration then the later part was written once the frustration was resolved. I hope to keep it as a reminder that I have the power to identify the feeling and to create the desired outcome despite the emotions bubbling deep within.

FRUSTRATED RESOLVE

Tidal waves of frustration crashing through my veins

Hammering so consistent, undoing me at the seams

Coursing with resolve to bring its structure down

Falling deeper into an abyss of regret

Forgetting how his smile beams

How much longer must I withstand the sadness?

I would like to forget

Trying hard to calm the anger that lurks within

Down to my knees before crashing to the ground

Begging the sun to warm my soul so when I turn to meet his gaze

I can feel compassion in my heart, but as is always true

The next moment could be the end or again we can begin

I think to myself the power I have, my strength to see this through

I turn and see a knowing smile on his face,

The smile that says "I'm sorry, I love you".

CONSUMED BY FLAMES

DEPRESSION'S VOICE:

You think you can get rid of me. I love how desperate you sound here but I am not a fan of the whole strength thing you are trying to end with.

CONSUMED BY FLAMES

Longing for more than the flames that consume me, searching for redemption that will finally remove me. My tears like cinders from a firework exploding, raining down from the sky, turning into hot glowing lava killing the living around me. Then as a spectator the sky stands witness to my fiery display sending clouds to come rescue me, soaking me in soothing comfort, whispering melodies leaving me but a small smolder. Somehow from the pit of the fire I will rise up and walk again among the living leaving the ashes of the past to be consumed by death.

SHATTERED

DEPRESSION'S VOICE:

I have convinced you to believe you are broken beyond repair. Yes, Hasty, be sure to warn everyone how miserably demonic you are. No need to start again... take my hand, babe, I will be your reality.

SHATTERED

The image I have tried to create lies shattered on the floor

Broken images staring back and taunting me

The me I aimed to be laughing at my failure

Exposing the self that hid behind the mirror

Throwing the broken pieces out the door

Recreating the person I think I should be

Realizing I haven't got a prayer

Because you have seen me far too clear

I turn to you exposed and naked

Looking for a reason I should start again

Barely holding on

Trying to repair the despair that has started creeping in

As I watch your face and then your heart comprehend the view

You were duped into believing I offered up reality

And even though you had every reason to turn and walk away

You walked over all the broken pieces

Joyful in the reality of the true me

CRUSHING CONSUMPTION

DEPRESSION'S VOICE:

YES! You have a talent for desperation.   I am the nothingness you seek; I am the voice within calling you away from those deceptive smiles seeking you out. Run from the light my dear, Hasty, let me devour you.

CRUSHING CONSUMPTION

I sit alone contemplating the numbness that threatens to consume me. Overwhelmed at the crushing consumption of it all. Even the darkness, full of dread, promises to be overcome by the nothingness that dwells within. Your voice, your smile, your understanding eyes scarcely breaks through the wall where emotions are lined up to die!

STORMS OF SELF SABOTAGE

Frantically running from the whimpering in my mind

I search for a way to stifle the doubt crushing me like a wave.

There is a light somewhere around here

I know because I have seen it before

Bursting like sunlight where only midnight used to live.

Severely lacking perspective of any normal kind

I search giant open caverns leading to and from my heart like a cave.

There is love somewhere around here

I know because I have glimpsed it before

Overflowing like lava where only sand used to live.

Recklessly disregarding any compliments I may find

I search longingly for the song the will free my dancing soul.

There is contentment somewhere around here

I know because I have felt it before

Intensifying like a storm where only calm used to live.

Fervently squashing the self-confidence I so sparingly mined

STORMS OF SELF SABOTAGE

I search everlasting that last vestige of tenacity I can muster to save.

There is faith somewhere around here

I know because I have had it before

Brilliant and sparkling like diamonds where only coal used to live.

Despairingly I reach for clarity but remain despondently blind

I search for the sight that lingers maddeningly out of reach

There is trust somewhere around here

I know because I have believed in it before

Solidly built like a mountain where only the tumultuous sea used to live

KISS MY SOUL

DEPRESSION'S VOICE:

Trust me, your heart isn't the only one that can hear you. I plan on pronouncing a sentence but it isn't one that you will come back to life from. I am dying to quench your desire to be devoured.

KISS MY SOUL

Constantly seeking bluer skies over horizons left unexplored

Losing track of the clear places in my mind

Marching at a never ending pace, longing for rest

Down for the count, longing for revival

Desperate for beauty to kiss my soul back to life.

Relentlessly looking back at the past trying to catch up with me

Keeping count of the miles I have been running

Marching to a beat that only my heart can hear

Down for the count, longing for revival

Desperate for beauty to kiss my soul back to life.

All too frequently I have started to let sorrow define me

Picking treacherous paths hoping they will devour me

Kneeling at the base of the throne for a sentence to be pronounced

Down for the count, longing for revival

Desperate for beauty to kiss my soul back to life.

THE ROOMS WITHIN

HASTY'S VOICE:

I realized one morning, as I was getting ready for work, that I felt.....content. It was odd for me to feel that way but even more odd that it had lasted a few days. I tried to figure out what the word "content" even meant. Secure, satisfied, confident, relaxed, peaceful I suppose. For me, I think it really means I am not actively over thinking anything, analyzing someone or what they said; in short, I am not actively worrying. I am emotionally content.

Searching myself for old familiar feelings

Emotions attached to fond memories

I believe them to be misplaced

Since they have been neglected for so long

In the solitude, I so often try to avoid

I travel hallways looking for this familiar room

Along the meandering corridors are

Cracked open doors containing various things

A place where long ago dreams make their home

Begging for help as if held prisoner all this time

Dreams left slumbering lazily in a peaceful sleep

THE ROOMS WITHIN

Desires better left undisturbed
Locked away under their blankets of cobwebs
Before long I find a well-worn doorknob
It leads to a room where the core of me is stored
As I sit in the quiet of this memory room
I see pictures of people hanging on the wall
Beautiful pictures of people I love
And cracked pictures of people who have hurt me
I have filled this room with meaningful items
A blanket my mom made, a stool my dad painted
A stuffed bunny from my sister, a valentine's from my husband
Regret likes to hide under the bed in this room
I let regret alone because she can be so full of misery
There is a bookshelf full of books filled with stories
My book of values and how they came to be
My book of faith and the stories that shaped thee
Books on love, on heartaches, on playful memories
My favorite book is my book of maps
Maps I have drawn to remind me not only where I have been
But places I would like to visit, the destinations I hope I find
The roads that will fulfill the dreams still awake within me
I love this room because it reminds me of who I am
It reminds me of why I am, and gives me the strength
To continue to be the person I sat out to be
To be passionately full of love to be beyond merely content

I'M NOT BROKEN

DEPRESSION'S VOICE:

That's right get mad. Your friends can't help you. You are NOT broken; you are crazy, and I am working on proving it to you.

I'M NOT BROKEN

They keep telling me I'm not ok
That something is broken inside of me
Friends telling me they don't know how to fix me
That they no longer know how to help me
Since when is that ok? Denying responsibility
I have my issues, I have many, and we can pick any one
But I am fairly sure that all those near and dear to me
Those I let close enough to see all of me
Those I warned but still wanted to know me
That is when it became ok…to simply let them see me
I take responsibility for the choices I have made
Choices and decisions made with a few regrets
That teach me, mold me, shape me into me
I am not broken, I am not broken, I am not broken
I do not need friends who feel they must fix me
Grouping ourselves into unusual obscurity
Personality disorders trying to label our mind
Like racial profiling labels our appearance
People changing, people blaming, people…
Stopped trying to listen, to understand, to love
We are beautifully unique, we have differences
We share who we are and take responsibility for ourselves
But communication between two people
Well….that requires shared responsibility
Two people committing, listening, and acting in a shared process
So if I am broken, then the rest of the world is broken with me

TEARING INTO SILENCE

DEPRESSION'S VOICE:

You give way too much control to your friends which is awesome. I mean, seriously, if I wasn't so bent on destroying you, I would tell you to snap out of it.

TEARING INTO SILENCE

Tearing into silence
Falling from perfection
Leaving me to silently fall into the lonely abyss
Your words mean everything yet they destroy me
Your silence unbearable, meant to unhinge me
Controlling me, changing me,
Seeking something that isn't inside of me.
I want to flee, to leave, to disembark this journey
To find a place where I am free from the disjointed harmony
For now I am imploding, waving the white flag
Please don't remember
The words, the looks, the tears
Streaking paragraphs down my face
Speaking unpublished volumes.
Exercise the memories
Where all our demonized characters dance
Burn them all up leaving them smoldering in the past
We fight, bicker, blame, and deny
There is no hope for honesty
So I flee out the back
Landing in the stairwell
Slumped up in a corner
Waiting for the next door to open
What is done is done…
What is done is done…
What is done is done…
What is done can't be undone.

UNSPOKEN MOMENTS

UNSPOKEN MOMENTS

Longing for a truth that never existed

For words that will never grace your lips

For sentiments that will never be born

Except for the life they have in my mind

Like shadows that vanish in the light

        The moments pass quietly unspoken.

FINALLY FOUND

DEPRESSION'S VOICE:

AHHHHHH   I HATE THIS!!!
You can't get rid of me that easily; medication won't make me disappear, just makes my job a little bit harder.   Don't start celebrating… I am not done dancing with you yet.

FINALLY FOUND

Rocking gently in this little boat of mine

Despite the crashing waves

Despite the raging sea all around me

Calm and collected, relaxed and content

Embracing parts of me long ago forgotten

It feels so beautiful to finally find this part of me

Politely responding to the emotional misgivings

Waving goodbye to negativity as if just a passer-by

Finding grace in the storms, finding substance in the mist

Finally finding and embracing this part of me

Perspective coming into focus

Perception no longer eluding me

Letting cruelty slip back into a long overdue slumber

Letting my soul breathe a gigantic sigh of relief

Finding and embracing, finally, this part of me

IF ONLY TRUST WAS EASIER

I went out with friends last night and had an amazing time. A group of maybe 15 people went to Dave & Busters and ate dinner together and then played games. It was actually really nice to have everyone get along, joke and laugh. But I had a bad dream about it last night.

I was getting ready to go out to Dave & Busters. I was talking to my daughter about her dinner plan's, I was fussing about what to wear when I realized nothing fit but this horrible cover up dress. On my way everyone kept texting me that they couldn't make it. I went only because I hadn't heard from a few people. When I got there everyone who canceled was sitting with someone else who had invited them, they didn't smile or even look my direction. I sat with two people I didn't even know who asked me polite questions. As they were listening to me talk they whispered something to each other and wrote me a note and left. The note said, "We are terribly sorry, we find you irrelevant, boring and overall just plain whiny...Life is too short." I glanced at the table where all my friends sat and some were rolling their eyes, some where laughing at me, some were just shaking their head sadly. I sat by myself and noticed and elderly overweight woman walking towards me wearing the same cover up dress I was wearing when I woke up.

Seriously, after any social event I dwell on all the verbal and physical cues I observed from those I interact with through out the night. I suck all the joy out of the laughter and hugs and love I shared and focus on all the not so pleasant things I may or may not have interpreted correctly. Does this make me crazy? I think so because I literally have to force myself into the next social activity.

One of the many things my dad taught me to do was to read people. He taught me the importance of listening and watching.

IF ONLY TRUST WAS EASIER

He said you will find out more about a person by watching how they relate to others and how they spend their time than you will learn listening to what they are saying directly to you. For instance, when listening to the descriptive speech people use you can tell whether someone needs to improve their self-esteem, whether they are impulsive extroverts, or if they like rules or have a tendency to rewrite the rules. For example, I know when my boss is stressed because he automatically begins to rub his temple. You can tell if someone is interested in what you are saying, are uncomfortable with a topic, if they are stressed or worried, if they are lying or avoiding. Most of us read people. We watch their eyes, their mouth, their hands, even their stance. Combine visual cues with verbal cues and you have an entire story reinforcing your view of the situation.

Here is the problem as I see it, our brains interpret the things we see and hear around us. We don't always interpret things correctly. Because our brains have to create shortcuts in order to quickly assess situations it can make mistakes. Our brains create patterns even when patterns may not actually exist.

Thinking about my dream I feel like I want to be oblivious to just trust people on the most basic level. And then it hit me, I don't trust. I think all the lessons my dad taught me are valid and can be used in a good way. However, I think because I don't trust anyone these things get the best of me. They say the happiest people trust others. If my brain could actually trust maybe I could interpret all the things I read differently. If only I can teach my brain trust…. If only….

IF ONLY TRUST WAS EASIER

DEPRESSION'S VOICE:

Well you have this right. You can't trust yourself as long as you've got me around. Trust is a stupid word if you ask me. Everyone wants it but nobody knows how to give it. Some people are more trustworthy than others but this is one of those "no person is perfect" things. Easy, easy, easy to use against people.

IF ONLY TRUST WAS EASIER

If only I could trust you

but there is a lack of eye contact

when you look in the mirror

the way you halfheartedly commit to

the conversations we have

If only I could trust you

to stop hurting yourself

to stop the incessant need to condemn yourself

the way you warp all the good ideas

turning them into jealousy and fear

If only I could trust you

but you don't respect me, support me, confide in me

how can I even begin to trust others

if I can't first trust you?

If only......I can just trust me.

FICTIONAL PLAYGROUND

DEPRESSION'S VOICE:

Hasty, you are so cute here thinking there is a difference between reality and fiction. You love to try to be all "girl power"... so gross.

FICTIONAL PLAYGROUND

Last night I tossed and turned

Thinking, solving, rethinking, resolving

Even in light slumber I can't run fast enough

I can't get away from the words that keep forming

Words, sentences, paragraphs, thoughts, ideas

They chase me relentlessly, persistently

In my dreams they manifest threateningly

drowning me, burning me, torturing me

They are the ghosts that end up haunting me

The tornadoes I spend all night hiding from

The killers I run from endlessly

The loved ones I can never quite save

I awake groggily to a new day

Jump in the shower to wash all the stories away

While fiction has the night time to play

My autobiography owns the day!!!

MY EMOTIONAL CONSTELLATION

HASTY'S VOICE:

Have you ever had to pee so bad you actually have trouble peeing? Well that is what writing is like for me. I have so much to say sometimes that I have to just sit and relax a moment. Like a muscle the brain starts to relax and then the words start pouring out. I started this journal to sort through my feelings. What I have learned is that emotion comes first...I have been writing emotionally. Feeling is secondary, writing helps me begin to feel a certain way about the emotions. Anyway, since this was on my mind I wrote the following:

MY EMOTIONAL CONSTELLATION

I am seeing a pattern emerge
As I sit here reading and writing my words
Like a constellation in the sky
My emotions move, they change
Sometimes slowly like an evolving season
Sometimes spinning at hurricane speeds
In the very beginning, before the patterns
The words seem scattered and distant
Like a ping pong ball in my head
They are hard to catch, to reign in
Like horses that got loose from their pen
I sit staring at my screen, my fingers poised
Waiting for my brain to make a connection
So many emotions to sort out
Lurking eagerly just under the surface
Screaming like children for their chance to be heard
In this moment I am the master
I alone get to pick my emotional destiny
My poised fingers begin to type
Ready to release passion from its irrational prison
Ahhh…. yes finally, the thoughts begin to stream
Rationality begins to surface when words are finally found.
And through all this, time and time again
I am seeing a pattern emerge
As I sit here reading and writing my words.

A SURPRISE VISIT

DEPRESSION'S VOICE:

I am not a visitor, I am a permanent fixture. Get it straight, Hasty; you are my prisoner. The only one you are fighting is me and I will win. Just relax and let your head and heart listen to me. Stop fighting, I will win eventually.

A SURPRISE VISIT

This unwelcome, unannounced emotional state

The one I am entertaining at this very moment

The one that makes me panic inside

The one suffocating me, blinding me

Amplifying everything inside of me

A few heart-broken sad minutes tick by

My sanity tossed around on an emotional sea

A fated shipwreck inevitable inside of me

A question with a greedy appetite is born

Deafening repetition, inescapable interrogation

Is it my head or my heart that feels so deserted?

Blaming each other for the disappointment

Hurling accusations of weakness, of insufficiency

Does the response even matter?

Will it end this tug of war raging on in me?

Regardless, the question remains begging for a solution

Is it my head or my heart? Is it my head or my heart?

TRUST?

DEPRESSION'S VOICE:

Don't trust her!

TRUST?

I always knew I had problems with trust

Doesn't everyone?

My friends tell me I need to have a little faith in them

This makes me stressed and confused

Now my therapist tells me I have trust issues

I am not sure if I should trust her

UNWELCOME SOLITUDE

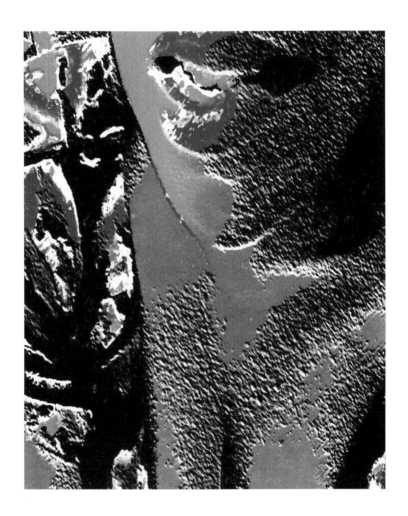

DEPRESSION'S VOICE:

I am your silence, Hasty. Come and let me hold you; let's talk. You have been trying to get away from my voice lately but you know you miss me... you need me.

UNWELCOME SOLITUDE

The silence unsettles me

I could never make it my home

Sometimes words fail me

And thoughts hide frozen and numb

The outside world is missing

Biting its tongue, abandoning me

I am not one to enjoy quiet solitude

It taunts me, surrounds me

Imprisons and suffocates me

Is it the world ignoring me?

Or am I avoiding the world?

Suffocated by tranquility

My ears yearn for meaning

Strangled by it, consumed by it

Tied up and bound by it

The silence unsettles me

I could never make it my home

IT'S COMPLICATED

DEPRESSION'S VOICE:

It isn't complicated, Hasty. You humans always love to complicate things with your ego and emotion. My job would be easier if you would just stop fighting to complicate things.

IT'S COMPLICATED

The simplicity melted away

It dissolved leaving pieces

Broken into fragments along the way

What was once so easy

Has become burdensome

It shouts its frustrated resolve

Through a megaphone of indifference

What was once a simple love

Has found itself stuck in a web

Of unshared hopes and dreams

Has found itself abandoned

With a one way ticket to…

It's complicated.

MELANCHOLY MADNESS

DEPRESSION'S VOICE:

See, it's so simple. You will disappear and you will be forgotten so just let go. Stop holding on and just let me dance you into eternity.

MELANCHOLY MADNESS

I feel lost and abandoned in time

A world without signs, directionless

No vocabulary can describe

Emotions out of sync

Relentless in their beat

Marching onward, inward, outward

Stirring up a mind full of crazy

Ready to feed on all the perpetual misery

Like a flock of seagulls

Scanning the horizon for the flaming sun

Scorching all that remains of the rot

Drying up the decay before it can be sought

Emotions menacing, staggering, drunk on deceit

Mastered by self-pity waiting to destroy

Those fairy tale stories of happiness and joy

Feelings neglected strangled by a rope

Hung from rafters like smoke from a fire

Evaporating before anyone is any wiser

The truth is what makes life sad

We will disappear in a flash

And be forgotten

Just like all the other stars before us.

CALL IT FATE

DEPRESSION'S VOICE:

Not crazy about you labeling me with words like "destiny", "providence", or "fate." I found you, not them. I am the stealthy killer stalking you. Get it into your head, Hasty. I deserve the credit for your destruction not them.

CALL IT FATE

Destiny

Providence

Fate

They find you

When they want to find you

They attach to you

When they have decided to attach to you

They create you at the same time they destroy you

They are silent in their capture

Smart with their disguise

Abundant in their strategies

Never failing to bend you to their will

BREATHING CONTRADICTION

DEPRESSION'S VOICE:

You really are of two minds aren't you ... hehehehehe

BREATHING CONTRADICTION

I am great

Except when I am not

I am strong

When I'm tired of being weak

I am brave

With a measure of fear

I am logical

Unless it's irrational

I am conceited

But mostly insecure

I am mindful

Of my obliviousness

I am everything

Bordering on nothing

I am alone

Surrounded by the world

LAST I KNEW

DEPRESSION'S VOICE:

You like these images, Hasty? Do you like the picture I am painting for you? Say goodbye. You don't need time because time will just keep hurting you.

LAST I KNEW

Once upon a time

I was lying on the shore

Listening to the waves

The seagull and their songs

The winds whispering flow

I believed in the future

I hoped for tomorrow

I longed to make a difference

Once upon a time

I was sitting under a tree

Listening to children play

The leaves rustling

The Cicadas harvesting summer

I didn't think about the future

I hoped for nothing

I was holding on to the moment

Last I knew

I was drowning in a stream

Listening to the passing world

The coolness taking my breath

The water washing over me

Thinking of the past

Hope eluding me

       Saying goodbye to time

SLEEPING HEART

HASTY'S VOICE:

I have days, like today, when I wake up feeling empty and sad. I have a beautiful life, I believe in a God of strength, I have an amazing family, and I am surrounded by friends. So why? I feel like my heart just ups and leaves and my brain is left wallowing in pity and fear. Today I am spiraling down and I am searching for a life line. Depression is exhausting and it is worse when you let it exhaust somebody else. There is something I realize even despite the despair, that this will pass, that I am a slave to thousands of chemical soldiers who would love nothing but to tear me down. Time is on my side....I just have to wait patiently.

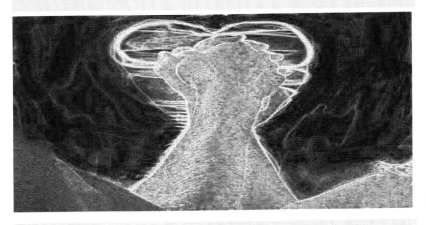

DEPRESSION'S VOICE:

Wait...
Did you just call me by name? For a smart girl you sure are dumb. You can't be more patient than me. I am more than just a chemical imbalance; I am the Demon that lives underneath your eyelids haunting your dreams; I am the warrior stealing your joy each day.
You have a beautiful life? You believe in God? You haven't prayed in awhile so you could have fooled me. I am holding fast to you, Hasty. You can't just leave this dance.

SLEEPING HEART

Heart slept in today

Tired, worn out, feeling used

Brain doesn't like to be left alone

He talks to himself and makes up stories

Brain becomes melancholy when he is alone

Brain knows how fragile heart is

Brain tries to protect Heart

He tries to help her pace herself

Give a little less and last a bit longer he says

But Heart is stubborn

Like a child who doesn't understand "no"

Brain convinces himself while she is away

That Heart cares for everyone but him

Why else would she run top speed

With no thought as to leaving him

But Brain needs Heart

He hates life when she is away

So he will just have to kill time

Overanalyzing everything that comes his way

CYRING RAIN

DEPRESSION'S VOICE:

That's right, Hasty, keep in time with me. Let's just dance, follow my lead.

CYRING RAIN

I can't see past the rain

It is shooting straight down

Blinding everything from sight

I see your face

I think you are speaking

But I can't hear past the downpour

I can make out your hands

Reaching desperately towards me

But the puddles are too deep

It has been raining too hard

For way too long

I know if I don't move

I will drown

But the deluge feels good

It comforts me

It promises to sweep me away

In a deep torrential stream

From the moments that came with life

Delivering me from time

To something new

To a place filled with oceans

Of eternity.

SCREAMING STATIC

DEPRESSION'S VOICE:

Nobody cares. All you have is me. Gift me with your screams of agony because I am hungry and tonight you are feeding me.

SCREAMING STATIC

Her screams are silent

A super charged storm

Discharging electricity

Raging seas churning down deep

Apocalypse ready to claim her

People pass by without a glimpse

Unaware of the torture

Holding her captive

Withholding happiness that feeds her

Screams ring loud and clear

Deafening only her own ears

Abandoned with the sound of her own agony

She lies invisible to the world around her

Until only shards remain of her spirit

And all that is left for her to hear is a silent static

THE PAIN OF SILENCE

DEPRESSION'S VOICE:

There you go again, Hasty. Calling me by another name. I am the silence that accompanies you.

THE PAIN OF SILENCE

In the beginning it was the silence

That held her in its arms

Embracing her body

Consoling her and absorbing her pain

Making promises to protect her

Eventually it was the silence

That stole her breath

Robbing her of words

Holding on to her secrets

Eventually it was the silence

That trapped her mind

Tormented her thoughts

And restricted her heart

In the end it was the silence

That imprisoned her

Stole her freedom

And pilfered her life

SEARCHING FOR PURPOSE

DEPRESSION'S VOICE:

What, no? There are no new opportunities, just death waiting for you, so stop these ridiculous poems about strength and pay attention to our dance. Stop spending time with your friends. The only remedy is isolation.

SEARCHING FOR PURPOSE

I was left drifting

In a turbulent sea

Purpose lost

My thoughts

Tidal waves

Of destruction

Head above water

Fighting the depth

Pulling at me

I cling to endurance

My strong capacity

To hold my breath

Until the waves

Begin to carry me

Safely towards

New opportunities

A DRESSED UP HEART

DEPRESSION'S VOICE:

Stop being sappy. Nobody cares about how you feel and this is only making you look weak and, well, quite frankly my dear, crazy.

A DRESSED UP HEART

I have an exposed heart
I was born that way
Everyone can see it
Everyone can touch it
It's on display everyday
When I was young
I cried a lot, alone
My feelings always hurt
One day
I made a mask
Specifically for my heart
It had sequins, glitter
Feathers, and stickers
Rainbows and lots and lots of glue
It fit my heart perfectly
And hid my pain well
Nobody could see my heart
My fears hid inside my silent tears
And when I was alone
I would take off the mask
Bandage myself up
Novocaine the hurts
And move on
Or so I thought
As I sat looking at the heart
Exposed without the mask
I realized it was bloody
Bruised, beat to a pulp
By hiding its pain
It never healed
It was crying to be saved
I realized I had ignored it
Hid it from myself
And now it was on its last heartbreak

MY PRISON SHELTER

DEPRESSION'S VOICE:

I will admit you had me concerned, ignoring me so easily. But I knew you couldn't stay away. You need me and, yes, you are lonely without me. Now take my hand and let's begin this dance again.

MY PRISON SHELTER

I tried so hard to escape
The prison inside my head
The thoughts condemning me
The noise screaming at me
The tormented bits and pieces
Got used to torturing me
Then I realized I was free
The voices a part of history
For a while I smiled content
But then I felt numb
Dare I say lonely?
So today I search earnestly
For its entrance
For a way back in
My thoughts feel icy
Heavy and unmoving
Stuck suffocating
As I search for ways
To rescue them
From the loneliness
They've endured
No longer tended to
Is it possible I miss them?
Is it true?
That now this prison
Has become my shelter too?

PIECEMEAL SOULS

DEPRESSION'S VOICE:

I don't like you sharing your feelings because it could backfire on me.

PIECEMEAL SOULS

These pages reflect
Images of me
Shattered pieces
For the world to see

Parts of my life
The smiles and the frowns
Gifts of emotion
To other piecemeal souls

Connections felt
Consequences dealt
Lessons learned
Temptations conquered

Disappointments shed
Confessions freed
Ambiguity leaked
In formatted phrases

I'm automatic in verse
It's my addiction
My ideas unleashed
On the world around me

TRIPPING ON PIECES

DEPRESSION'S VOICE:

Oh, Hasty, this is beautiful. I nearly cried (as if that were possible). When you listen to me you really listen to me. Now just hang in here with me and we can finish this dance more quickly.

TRIPPING ON PIECES

I tripped randomly

Stumbling upon

Something resembling me

Or at least a part of me

I couldn't really tell

Because darkness

Cried so loudly

I couldn't think

So I covered my ears

Screaming obscenities

Asking it to stop

Finally noise deafened me

Quiet began to smother me

I looked around disjointedly

Left wondering

If there were more

Broken pieces to find

BORN BROKEN

DEPRESSION'S VOICE:

Again, this is me. I have you, Hasty. There is no love great enough to save you. You are alone here with me.

BORN BROKEN

There is a deep disappointment

Residing in a lonely soul

Hearts born emotionally broken

That no amount of love can fix

There is sadness so cold and so deep

No medication can cure

No arms warm enough can heat

"I love you" passes invisibly by

Unable to be grasped

Unwilling to be heard

This heart of mine

Is like a magnet

It repels all things

That try to speak truth into me

SWALLOWING SORROW

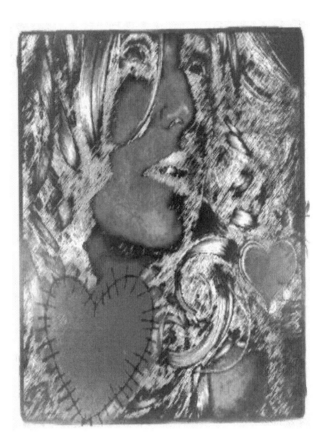

DEPRESSION'S VOICE:

Yes, say goodbye to everyone. Do them a favor and just finish this dance. They don't need you; they don't spend the time with you that I do. Come on baby, let me show you someplace more deserving of a soul such as yours.

SWALLOWING SORROW

I awakened appreciating
How happy you will be
With the absence of me
And as I swallow the sorrow
I let the joy of your potential
Reassure the doubts
Easing so comfortably
Into the bones that secure me
The time you spent reassuring me
Redirected to opportunities
Knocking unanswered because of me
I kneel on the shoreline
Looking at a horizon full of promises
And there I stuff my feelings in a bottle
Full of messages of goodwill
Full of hopes and dreams I wish for you
Then I push you out to sea
Where I watch and pray
You are swept away
Into uncharted waves of happiness
And peaceful currents take you
To all the places you dream to see

VINEGAR WORDS

VINEGAR WORDS

Vinegar words distilled
Laced with powdered cyanid
Poisoning hopeful optimism
With random acts of lemony yawns

Spacious inquisitive forums
Speak in opportunistic flows
Into rivers of conscious patterns
Upon rocks and boulders below

People leave, they just do
They say goodbye, and they move on
They clear you from their eyes
And there's nothing you can do

Hands in pockets, watching
As life switches story lines
No fight left to grab it back
Inevitability was in all the signs

It's just too bad it had to end
With frustrated feelings unresolved
With a canyon filled with apologies
Echoing deaf upon our ears

The words that crashed into the wall
Had nowhere else to go
And will remain till the end of time
As pictured graffiti of our friendships fall

WHEN THERE IS NOTHING LEFT

DEPRESSION'S VOICE:

You are making this too easy. Burn all your bridges, honey. This is fun to watch. Your drama is the kind I love to watch.

WHEN THERE IS NOTHING LEFT

I keep crying, you keep screaming
Wishes running over, ruining our plans
My emotions you keep bending
You never give me a chance
Constantly making me feel like
There's nothing left to give

You twist every word, every thought
I ever even dreamed to have
Shredding all my dignity
Like I never had any at all
You keep trying to drown me
Only to bury me in the ground

When the day comes, I lie in slumber
As I dread the things you'll say to me
Would you feel better, live better
If I just packed my stuff to leave?
Our hearts left broken, words unspoken
My heart bruised and forever incomplete

FOREVER FLAWED

DEPRESSION'S VOICE:

The truth can be found by listening to me. Stop thinking, just listen, just feel, just dance.

FOREVER FLAWED

I look in the mirror, at reflections
Staring into eyes, looking into eyes
Searching for something, anything
The source for why this image cries

I lay in my breath, holding onto it
Seeking the air, questioning the air
Needing new breath, new life
The staleness of my own I cannot bare

I rest my hand on my heart, and cry
It sings to a restless depressing beat
I sit and listen to its story unfold
I try to understand the rhythm it speaks

I search my brain, get lost in thoughts
Over-analyze, over-think, beliefs in my head
My very worst quality, the life in my mind
The best I can do is tuck the truth in and put it to bed

BREATHING MUD

DEPRESSION'S VOICE:

This is so good, it is perfect actually. Don't stop just keep writing, keep crying...it won't be long now.

BREATHING MUD

It's my fault

My carelessness

I blame myself

For all of it

The logic

Disappears

Without a trace

And I am left

Wandering

Alone in the dark

It's a muddy dark

The kind that clings to you

The kind that covers you

And dries so hard

Leaving its residue

I want to lie down

To breathe it in

To let it fill my insides

Until part of the earth

Is all I am

TRAPPED INSIDE

DEPRESSION'S VOICE:

It is too late to fight now. I have destroyed all the fighting parts of you. Hidden them so deep you will never find them.. Just let go... give in... DANCE with me!!!

TRAPPED INSIDE

You hide inside
In a place I can't find
Your words trapped
In a field of mines
Afraid your thoughts
Might be caught
And ensnared
Ready to be stripped
And hung to dry
Naked and bare
Waiting to be judged
I fight for control
To overcome your silence
To pry the feelings
From the grave
You have greedily dug
I fight to save
You from hiding any part
Of the person
I have come to love

SILENCE WITHOUT SOUND

DEPRESSION'S VOICE:

Oh yes, this is how the dance feels when you just let me lead. I can give you the happiness you are looking for, the silence without sound. Just concentrate on the music of our feet dancing to these final heart beats.

SILENCE WITHOUT SOUND

Your kiss sends me flying

Above natures golden leaves

Your words send me diving

Into waters full of mystery

But my heart keeps stopping

Worried I've flown too far

Worried I dove too deep

In the moments without a beat

I can hear the demons call

They know me by name

They mimic your voice

I don't deserve to be happy

The voices are harsh, berating

Asking why someone could possibly

Love such a troubled soul as me

End the end I fall, in the end I drown

Because I flew too high they said

Because I dove too deep they cried

Taunting my feeble humanity

They save me from the sky

They protect me from the sea

And they promise me the one thing

They know I really crave, need

They promise me silence without sound

A SEASON OF DEPRESSION

DEPRESSION'S VOICE:

Spare me this wishy-washy weakness turn strength bologna. I am not a season dear, I am here until your end; however long that may be.

A SEASON OF DEPRESSION

My mood changes direction
Blowing leaves from their perch
Beautiful colors of perfection
Flowing in Fall's breezy search

I listen to the symphony
The rustling change of my nature
No longer prone to resiliency
Enters a season of danger

Clouds of depression cover the sky
Shadows of selfishness blanket the ground
Logic and reason take to the sky
While rationality mutes its sound

I feel the malicious majesty
Of my Fall turn Winter
The brutal travesty
That turns my heart so bitter

My body feels the transformation
As the world turns to stone
Under a snow laden foundation
Turning living flesh to frozen bone

GREY SHADES

HASTY'S VOICE:

When I accept who I am, start believing in myself, and begin to acknowledge I am a work of art constantly changing; I begin to see where I need to start. That place where loving myself begins.

GREY SHADES

I try to search for the opposite of me
But the image I seek keeps ghosting
I am grey shades built on blurry lines
They are infinite and hard to define
Trembling naked without any covers
I feel myself shivering from shame
How did I end up in this sinful space
What happened to the innocence
To the beautiful skin of my youth
Should I acknowledge the decay
To the festering, growing discontent
Should I ask the God to whom I pray
To lend me his eyes, to show me the way
I am sure in his eyes I would find
There is no opposite of me
I am grey shades built on blurry lines
That are infinite and hard to define
A body in a world of shifting shapes
I am changing spirit, an adaptation in time

DEPRESSION'S DANCE

My wicked depression

Smiles back at yours

For a while they dance

Amidst the storm

No fairytale lessons

No knight in shining armor

Just dark camaraderie

Leering at each other

Anger rages in the distance

Sadness cries its melodies

Happiness imprisoned

The joyful dead

Litter the ground

While our depression

Waltzes in time together

Across the floor

To a melancholy beat

27075406R00060

Made in the USA
Charleston, SC
02 March 2014